Dear Sis
Let's Walk This
Out Together

From My Heart to Yours: A 31-Day Devotional of
Faith, Hope, and Healing
Wives Edition

Dr. Tache' Vereen

Dear Sis: Let's Walk This Out Together — From My Heart to Yours:
A 31-Day Devotional of Faith, Hope, and Healing- Wives Edition

Unless otherwise noted, all Scripture quotations are taken from:
The Holy Bible, New Living Translation (NLT), copyright © 1996, 2004, 2015 by Tyndale House Foundation. Used by permission of Tyndale House Publishers, a Division of Tyndale House Ministries. All rights reserved.

Amplified Bible (AMP), copyright © 1954, 1958, 1962, 1964, 1965, 1987 by The Lockman Foundation. Used by permission. www.lockman.org

Book Cover & Layout Design: Abu Bakar Javed

Published by: DOC with TV LLC

Printed in the United States of America

www.docwithtv.com

ISBN: 979-8-9993418-1-5

Acknowledgments

First and foremost, all glory belongs to God—my Savior, my Anchor, my Everything! Without Him, none of this would have been possible. Thank You, Lord, for placing this devotional on my heart and for walking with me through every season of my life and marriage. You have been my strength, my guide, and my peace every step of the way.

To my husband, my partner in life and love, thank you. Your patience, encouragement, and unwavering support have allowed me to pour my heart into this devotional. Your love teaches me daily how-to walk-in grace, humility, and faith, and I am forever grateful for you.

To my friends and sister circle, thank you for being my sounding board, my cheerleaders, and my prayer warriors. Your encouragement and honesty have strengthened me as a wife, a woman of God, and a sister in Christ.

To my spiritual mentors and leaders, your wisdom, guidance, and prayers have shaped my journey and helped me grow in faith and in marriage. Your influence is woven into every word of this devotional.

And to every wife reading these pages, I wrote this for you. I see you, I understand your struggles, your joys, and your desire to grow closer to God and your husband. My prayer is that this devotional meets you where you are, strengthens your faith, and encourages you to keep walking in love, grace, and patience. You are never alone, Sis.

Table of Contents

Introduction

Dear Sis,

I wrote this edition of *Dear Sis* with you—yes, you, Wife—on my heart. Not just because I am a wife myself, but because I deeply believe in marriage and I long to see marriages not just survive, but thrive.

In these pages, I want you to feel like you have a sister in your corner—a sister who will cheer you on through every season of your marriage. Whether you're a newlywed learning your spouse's rhythms, a seasoned wife navigating new chapters, a wife fighting to hold on in a hard season, or one standing strong and thriving—I'm here, walking this out with you.

I know marriage is not always easy. As a wife, I have faced my own moments of joy, growth, sacrifice, and learning. And through it all, one truth remains: God must always be the head of your marriage. No one and nothing should ever take His place. When we trust Him fully—when we lean not on our own understanding but acknowledge Him in every decision, conflict, and celebration—He promises to direct our paths.

This devotional is my heartfelt way of reminding you that you are not alone. It's an invitation to pause, reflect, and hear your sister in Christ whisper, *"Sis, you've got this—and God's got you."*

So take a deep breath, open your heart, and let's walk this out together. Day by day. Hand in hand. Always with Him at the center.

"Trust in the Lord with all your heart and do not depend on your own understanding. Seek his will in all you do, and he will show you which path to take."
— Proverbs 3:5–6 NLT

With love and sisterhood,
Dr. Tache' Vereen

How to Use This 31- Day Devotional

This devotional is meant to be read one day at a time, but Sis, I want you to move at your own pace. Some days, God may have you pause and sit a little longer. Other days, you may feel ready to move forward. That's okay—follow His lead.

Here's how I recommend using this devotional each day:

- **Start with prayer.** Invite the Holy Spirit into your time and space. Pray over your heart and your marriage.

- **Read the Scripture.** Let the Word wash over you and your union—don't rush it.

- **Read the "Dear Sis" entry.** Picture me sitting with you—wife to wife—talking, listening, and sharing heart to heart.

- **Pray the prayer.** Use it as a starting point, then talk to God in your own words too. Bring Him your marriage, your spouse, and your own heart.

- **Reflect and worship.** Sit with the prompt. Journal your thoughts, prayers, and hopes for your marriage. Be still or worship—whatever you need. Look up the song suggestion and let the music minister to your soul and your home. Sometimes God speaks the loudest through a melody.

If you don't feel led to move to the next day—don't. Maybe God is doing something deep in you, your heart, or your marriage. Stay there. Let Him finish what He started. This isn't a checklist—it's a journey with Jesus, and your marriage is in His hands.

Let this devotional be your quiet place, your safe space, your soul refresh—and a gentle reminder that you are not walking this road alone.

And remember, Sis—I'm right here, wife to wife, cheering you on.

A Prayer of Blessing

Father,

In Jesus' name, I pray that You would cover my sister in Christ—her marriage and her home. I pray that as she reads, she encounters You deeply, and day by day she is being changed by Your power. Father, lead her step by step as she journeys through these pages. Wash her clean and make her whole in You.

I pray that she and her husband will become one, just as You designed—joined together, never to be separated. Keep them close, guard their hearts, and renew their minds. Draw them nearer to You, Father, so that their marriage reflects Your love and truth.

Father, I thank You that my sister would be revived, restored, and renewed by Your power. Open her eyes to see You at work in her marriage and her home. Open her ears to hear Your voice in the quiet places of her heart and within her relationship. May she become a safe place for her husband—a haven of love, grace, and strength.

Cover her, keep her, and bless her, Lord. In Jesus' name, Amen.

> *"Therefore a man shall leave his father and mother and be joined to his wife, and they shall become one flesh."*
> — **Genesis 2:24 (NKJV)**

Day 1:   Who Do They Say You Are?

Scripture:
*"When Jesus came to the region of Caesarea Philippi,
he asked his disciples, '
Who do people say that the Son of Man is?'"*
— *Matthew 16:13 NLT*

Dear Sis,

If you were to ask this same question about yourself to the people closest to you — your husband, your children, your family, your friends — what would they say?

Now, I'm not saying their words define you, because only Jesus gets the final say about who you are. But it does matter how we show up in our homes, Sis. Sometimes we get so busy, tired, and stretched thin that our tone can get sharp, our words can cut, and our attitude can shift before we even realize it.

But what if today, you paused and asked the Lord to help you see yourself honestly — through His eyes first, and then through the eyes of those you love?
Are you known as a safe place for your husband? Do your words build him up or tear him down? Is your home a haven or a battlefield?

This isn't to shame you — it's to remind you that you carry the light of Christ, even in your marriage. Your words, your patience, your smile — they can shift the atmosphere of your home.

So today, Sis, I encourage you to ask Jesus to help you walk out your true identity — not just who people *say* you are, but who *He says* you are: chosen, beloved, clothed in strength and dignity, a wise woman who builds her house.

You've got this. And I'm right here with you.

Prayer:
Lord, Shape My Reflection

Lord, thank You for calling me Yours. Help me to see myself through Your eyes and live out my identity as a wife who honors You. Teach me to speak life, to love deeply, and to reflect Your kindness in my home. Let my husband see Your love through my actions and my words. Shape me daily to be more like You. In Jesus' name, Amen.

Reflect and Worship

♫ Song Suggestion:
"Refiner"
— Maverick City Music

Sis, as you reflect on today's devotional, take a moment to worship with this song. Let the lyrics remind you that God is refining you daily, shaping you into who He says you are — not just who others say you are. *Look it up on your favorite music platform and let it speak to your heart today.*

Reflection Prompt:

Who do people say you are? Who does God say you are? Where can you show up more like Him in your marriage today?

Day 2: Take the Help

Scripture:
"So let us come boldly to the throne of our gracious God. There we will receive his mercy, and we will find grace to help us when we need it most."
— *Hebrews 4:16 NLT*

Dear Sis,

Take the help, Sis. You can't do this on your own — and you were never meant to.

I've learned over the years, through every season of my marriage, that I *need* God's help. I need His help to live a holy life, to love well, and to be the kind of wife my husband needs and my Father calls me to be.

I need His help when trust is tested. I need His help when I don't understand what He's doing in my marriage. I need His help when forgiveness feels hard, and patience feels impossible.

So I choose to take His help — every single day. And Sis, you can too. You don't have to carry the weight of your marriage on your own shoulders. You don't have to figure it all out alone.

Let God help you love your husband. Let Him help you forgive him, pray for him, respect him, be patient with him — and yes, submit to him with a heart that trusts *God* first.

Don't keep pushing through on empty. Come boldly to the throne. There's fresh grace waiting for you — right now, right here.

Prayer:
Lord, I Choose Your Help

Father, thank You for welcoming me to Your throne of grace. I come boldly, asking for Your help in my marriage. Help me love my husband the way You love me. Help me forgive quickly, pray faithfully, and walk in patience and respect. I can't do this on my own, but with You I have everything I need. In Jesus' name, amen.

Reflect and Worship

♪ Song Suggestion:
"Lord, I Need You"
— Matt Maher

Sis, as you reflect on today's devotional, pause to worship with this song. Let the words remind you that you don't have to carry it all alone — help is one prayer away. *Find this song on your favorite music platform and let it wash over you today.*

Reflection Prompt:

What burden have you been trying to carry by yourself? How can you let God help you love, forgive, or trust in your marriage today?

Day 3:   Listen and Find Life

Scripture:

"Come to me with your ears wide open. Listen, and you will find life.
I will make an everlasting covenant with you.
I will give you all the unfailing love I promised to David."
— Isaiah 55:3 NLT

Dear Sis,

Hallelujah. Sis, God wants to speak to *you* — about you. He wants to give you something that no one else can: an everlasting covenant and His unfailing love.

It's beautiful to have your sisters in Christ to lean on and encourage you — but only *God* can speak to you about who you truly are and about what He desires for your marriage.

When you spend time with your Father, come with your ears wide open and your heart soft and ready to listen. Get to that quiet place, beyond the noise of your fears, your worries, your own thoughts — and just *listen.*

God's promise is clear: when you listen, you *find life.* So today, Sis, slow down long enough to hear Him. Let Him speak life into you — and into your marriage.

Prayer:
Lord, Open My Ears

Father, thank You for loving me with an everlasting love. Open my ears to hear Your voice above all others. Quiet my heart so I can receive what You want to say to me and my marriage. Help me trust Your words and walk in the life You promised. In Jesus' name, Amen.

Reflect and Worship

♫ Song Suggestion:
: *"Speak to My Heart"*
— Donnie McClurkin

Sis, as you reflect on today's devotional, find a quiet moment to worship with this song. Let it remind you that God still speaks — and He wants to speak directly to your heart. *Look it up on your favorite music platform and let His words breathe life into you today.*

Reflection Prompt:

Where can you slow down this week to truly listen to God? What noise do you need to quiet so you can hear Him clearly?

Day 4:   A Prescription for Peace

Scripture:
"Don't worry about anything; instead, pray about everything. Tell God what you need, and thank him for all he has done. Then you will experience God's peace, which exceeds anything we can understand. His peace will guard your hearts and minds as you live in Christ Jesus."
— *Philippians 4:6–7 NLT*

Dear Sis,

Sis, this is a great prescription for life *and* for marriage. Why? Because when we take this prescription, we can be sure we'll experience something that only God can do in us — no matter what comes our way.

Marriage is beautiful, and I truly enjoy being married. But let's be real: there will be times when everything is going well — and out of nowhere, the enemy tries to poke his head into your marriage. But don't worry, Sis. Keep on loving your husband. Keep praying for him. Keep believing God for a breakthrough.

That's why it's so important for you, as a wife, to have a prayer life. Every single day, decide to bring it *all* to the Father — and leave it with Him. Trust that He will handle it all, in His way and His timing.

I'm realizing that the more I give it to God — and *leave it* with Him — the more I experience a peace like never before. And Sis, I'll keep taking this scripture as my prescription for my life and my marriage. I pray you do too.

Prayer:
✳ # Lord, Be My Peace ✳

Father, I ask You to cover my sister today. Cover her mind. Keep her, guide her, lead her, and help her. Open her eyes so she can see that Your Word is her daily prescription for a life free of worry. Holy Spirit, teach her how to pray and not give in to worry, so she can experience peace like never before. In Jesus' name, Amen.

Reflect and Worship

🎵 **Song Suggestion:**
"Lead Me On"
— Chandler Moore

Sis, as you reflect on today's devotional, take a moment to worship with this song. Let it remind you that God is leading you and covering you with a peace that passes all understanding. *Look it up on your favorite music platform and let it calm your heart today.*

Reflection Prompt:

What are some areas in your life where you truly need to stop worrying and give it to the Father? Can you picture yourself free from worrying about those things

Day 5:   Nothing Hidden

Scripture:

"Nothing in all creation is hidden from God. Everything is naked and exposed before his eyes, and he is the one to whom we are accountable."
— *Hebrews 4:13 (NLT)*

Dear Sis,

Sis, we can't hide anything from God — He sees it all. He lovingly exposes what we try to bury because He wants to heal us and make us whole. There's no need to pretend or cover up with Him — He already knows.

There was a time in my marriage when I had to truly surrender my heart to God. The hidden issues in my heart were becoming a barrier to how He wanted to use me in my home. In His gentle way, He showed me myself — and I had to make the choice daily to surrender my heart and those hidden issues to Him.

It didn't happen overnight. I had to keep laying it all down until I was free. And as I surrendered, I found the grace to forgive. It didn't always feel good, but looking back, I thank God that He exposed those dark places. Now my heart is lighter, my home is more peaceful, and I'm more available for God to use me as a vessel in my marriage and family.

Sis, don't be afraid to let Him search your heart. He wants you free so nothing can hinder what He wants to do in and through you.

Prayer: Lord, Expose My Heart

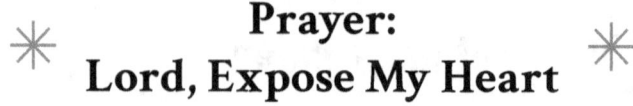

Father, in Jesus' name, I humbly ask You to expose anything in my sister's heart that may be hindering her from moving the way You desire. Show her the places You lovingly want to heal and change, so she can be a soft place for her husband and her family. Give her strategies and the strength to walk it out. In Jesus' name, Amen.

Reflect and Worship

🎵 **Song Suggestion:**
"Change Me"
— Tamela Mann

Sis, as you reflect today, let this song be your honest prayer. Invite God to purify and prepare you so you can be a vessel He can fully use in your marriage and home. *Look it up and let it wash over your heart.*

Reflection Prompt:

Do you want to be a vessel? What hidden thing is God asking you to surrender today?

Day 6:   Speak the New

Scripture:
"For I am about to do something new. See, I have already begun! Do you not see it? I will make a pathway through the wilderness. I will create rivers in the dry wasteland."
— Isaiah 43:19 (NLT)

Dear Sis,

Sis, I believe the Word of God — and I believe it for you too. There are times when, despite what you see, you have to declare and decree a *new thing* in your marriage and in your home. You have to speak God's Word over your marriage and believe Him to do what He promised.

I encourage you today: walk around your home and declare *new, new, new.* Speak *new, new, new* over your marriage. Get excited about it, Sis! Believe His Word. Praise God for it in advance.

I believe God is doing a new thing in your life, in your marriage, and in your family. I see it. I believe it. Keep speaking the new thing. Keep decreeing and declaring it over your home. Don't be moved by what you see — let God's Word move you.

His Word says He's making a pathway through the wilderness and rivers in the dry wasteland. Do you see it? Do you hear it? Are you receiving it? Will you walk in it? Let me tell you — *I am! Sis,* new looks good on me, and it looks good on you too.

Prayer: New Looks Good on Me

Father, I pray that You will remove the veil over my sister's eyes and cause her to see the new thing You are doing in her life, her marriage, and her family. As she dives into Your Word to gain strength and strategy, give her insight into what to speak over her home at the right time. Help her see the things that distract her and cause her to lose focus and faith — and help her overcome them by Your anointing and power. Lord, as she begins to speak *new* into her marriage and family, show her how to walk like it's already done. Help her to enjoy it. In Jesus' name, Amen.

Reflect and Worship

♫ Song Suggestion:
"Give Me Faith"
— Elevation Worship

Sis, play this song today and let it stir up fresh faith in you to believe for the new thing God is doing. Let it remind you to trust Him and speak His promises over your marriage and home. *Look it up on your favorite music platform and let it speak to your heart today.*

Reflection Prompt:

What "new thing" are you declaring and believing God for in your marriage and family? Write it down and speak it out loud today.

Day 7:   Never Stop Praying

Scripture:
"Never stop praying."
— *1 Thessalonians 5:17 (NLT)*

Dear Sis,

Prayer is important. This morning during our devotional time, I asked my oldest son, "Why do you think it's important to never stop reading and praying?" He said, "Because reading God's Word keeps your spirit from dying and keeps Jesus in your heart. Praying keeps you in constant conversation with God and keeps your spirit strong." Hallelujah for childlike wisdom!

Never stop praying. Keep reading God's Word. Wow — the wisdom that comes from our children! But think about it, Sis. If we choose to stop praying for our husbands, our children, and our homes — what might wither as a result? I don't want my faith to dry up and make room for the enemy's lies about my family.

Prayer is so important for a believer because it keeps us in conversation with our Father. One thing I've learned along my journey as a believer and as a wife is this: I *need* to pray. It's essential. I'm the one who sets my alarm for 6 a.m. daily so I can get up, pray, and spend time with God. I need it. I want to bring all my concerns to the Father and allow Him to pour back into me.

I never know what the day may hold, but I want to be prepared. Sis, I encourage you to find your quiet time — and stick with it. Decide today that you will never stop praying, no matter what.

Prayer: Never Stop

Father, Your Word encourages us to never stop praying. Help my sister find her time with You and commit to it, no matter what. Thank You for encouraging her heart as she comes to You with every concern for her marriage and her family. Remind her that prayer is essential — she can't live without it. Give her eyes to see the answers to her prayers, and let those answers fuel her faith to keep going, no matter what. In Jesus' name, Amen.

Reflect and Worship

♫ **Song Suggestion:**
"Made a Way"
— Travis Greene

Sis, let this song remind you that God still makes a way when there seems to be no way. Let it encourage you to keep praying and trusting that He hears every word. *Look it up on your favorite music platform and let it speak to your heart today.*

Reflection Prompt:

When can you set aside dedicated time to pray every day? Write it down and make the commitment to stick with it this week.

Day 8:   Pray Anyway

Scripture:
"Bless those who curse you. Pray for those who hurt you."
— Luke 6:28 (NLT)

Dear Sis,

Sis, let me tell you about a time when the enemy used someone to speak against my marriage. It bothered me deeply because all I ever wanted for that person was good. But they didn't want that for me and my marriage.

I took it to God in prayer — and He began to remind me of this very scripture. He showed me how I needed to pray for that person. Sis, let me be honest — blessing them was the last thing on my mind in prayer. It was hard. It felt unfair. But it was necessary.

I want to encourage you: this is doable. It's not easy, but it's possible. Did you notice the scripture doesn't say anything about how you'll feel about doing it? It doesn't mean your feelings don't matter — but it does mean you sometimes have to find a place for those emotions. My place is prayer.

I believe that when we choose to do what's right — even when it's hard — God will handle the rest. He'll take care of you and your marriage. So pray anyway. Bless anyway. Trust that God sees it all and He will take care of the rest. Trust Him to defend you, protect you, and bless you in ways you can't imagine.

Prayer:
Bless and Keep Me

Father, thank You for reminding me that when people hurt me, I can come to You. Help my sister bless those who curse her and pray for those who hurt her. Strengthen her heart to do what feels impossible and remind her that You see her sacrifice and her obedience. Bless her marriage, protect her family, and handle every battle on her behalf. In Jesus' name, Amen.

Reflect and Worship

♫ Song Suggestion:
"Forgiveness"
— Matthew West

Sis, listen to this song and let it remind you that forgiveness and blessing others doesn't make you weak — it makes you free. Let this song help you release what needs to be released to God. *Look it up on your favorite music platform and let it speak to your heart today.*

Reflection Prompt:

Who is God asking you to bless and pray for, even though it's hard? Write their name down and commit to pray for them this week.

Day 9:   Guided by His Word

Scripture:
"Your word is a lamp to guide my feet and a light for my path."
— Psalm 119:105 (NLT))

Dear Sis,

We need the Word of God. Hallelujah — praise God for His Word! It's so important to read it daily, to meditate on it, and to ask for wisdom and understanding. His Word will guide you, comfort you, and strengthen you when you feel empty or unsure.

Sis, you *need* the Word of God to encourage you, lead you, motivate you, and guide you in your marriage. When things get difficult, when misunderstandings come, when you're trying to love your husband in a season that feels hard — the Word will light your path.

Use God's Word to decree and declare blessings over your marriage. Speak life over your husband using Scripture. His Word is powerful enough to soften hearts, heal wounds, and bring new life into dry places.

I encourage you today: let His Word be the lamp that guides your feet through your home. Let it light up a path to your husband's heart and reveal the areas where God wants to use you to bring peace, healing, and unity. Hold tight to His Word — it will never fail you.

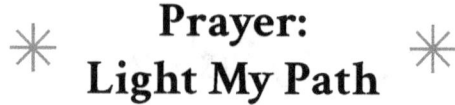

Prayer:
Light My Path

Father, guide my sister as she walks through Your Word. As she reads it, let knowledge, wisdom, and understanding spring up inside her and make her desire more of You. Shine Your light on every dark place in her marriage and in her home. Show her how to use Your Word to speak life, hope, and blessing over her husband. Let Your Word be her lamp and her strength every single day. In Jesus' name, Amen.

Reflect and Worship

♫ Song Suggestion:
"Fill the Room"
— — Michael Bethany & Jonathan Traylor

Sis, let this song remind you to invite God's presence to fill your home and your heart as you speak His Word over your life. *Look it up on your favorite music platform and let it speak to your heart today.*

Reflection Prompt:

Are there areas in your marriage where you need God's Word to light a path? Will you commit to partnering with Him so He can guide you and use you in your home?

Day 10:   Stay in His Presence

Scripture:
"You will show me the path of life; In Your presence is fullness of joy; In Your right hand there are pleasures forevermore."
— *Psalm 16:11 (AMP)*

Dear Sis,

When I wake up in the morning, I can't wait to get to my quiet place — my living room — so I can sit in God's presence, pray, and read His Word. Just like this scripture says, I know He will show me which path to take.

In His presence, I feel safe. I feel comforted, loved, filled with peace, and overflowing with joy. There's nothing like it. And Sis, in marriage, you will need this closeness with God more than ever.

Some days, you'll need Him to show you the path of forgiveness. Some days, you'll need Him to guide you into a new season with your husband, or teach you how to see your spouse in a fresh, grace-filled way. His presence has everything you need — wisdom, clarity, strength, and peace for your marriage.

Stay in His presence every day. Make time for it. Protect that time fiercely. He is so ready to pour out exactly what you need for your heart, your home, and your husband. Sis, there's fullness of joy waiting for you there — just receive it.

Prayer:
Show Me the Way

Father, thank You for the gift of Your presence. Draw my sister closer to You every single day. Fill her with Your peace, joy, and strength as she sits with You. Show her the paths she needs to take in her marriage — whether it's the path of forgiveness, patience, or learning her husband's heart in a new way. Lead her and love her so she can lead and love well in her home. In Jesus' name, Amen.

Reflect and Worship

♫ Song Suggestion:
"I Speak Jesus' (feat. Steve Musso)
— Charity Gayle

Sis, let this song cover your home, your heart, and your marriage with the power and presence of Jesus. *Take a moment to look it up on your favorite music platform and let it minister to your spirit today.*

Reflection Prompt:

What path is God showing you right now for your marriage? Where do you need His presence to guide you today?

Day 11:   Obedience Brings Victory

Scripture:

"But the Lord said to Joshua, 'Get up! Why are you lying on your face like this? Israel has sinned and broken my covenant! They have stolen some of the things that I commanded must be set apart for me. And they have not only stolen them but have lied about it and hidden the things among their own belongings. That is why the Israelites are running from their enemies in defeat. For now Israel itself has been set apart for destruction. I will not remain with you any longer unless you destroy the things among you that were set apart for destruction. Get up! Command the people to purify themselves in preparation for tomorrow. For this is what the Lord, the God of Israel, says: Hidden among you, O Israel, are things set apart for the Lord. You will never defeat your enemies until you remove these things from among you.'"
— Joshua 7:10–13 (NLT)

Dear Sis,

Sis, sometimes *we* are the reason we're not seeing victory. God gives us instructions for our marriages, our homes, and our hearts — but if we ignore Him, or drag our feet, or do it halfway — we block our own blessing. Look, I've been there. I remember when God told me to do what was right in my marriage — and I thought, Oh, I got this! I did the right thing... but with the wrong attitude. Then God whispered, *"Do what's right — with a good attitude!"* Whew! That felt like it cut straight through me.

I thought my actions alone would bring the breakthrough, but God saw my heart — and it wasn't right. So I repented and did it the *way He wanted* — and Sis, when I obeyed fully, I saw a change in my husband that only God could do. It pays to obey Him — all the way. I was crying and complaining about what I didn't see happening in my marriage, but I wasn't willing to *do it His way.* That lesson stays with me.

Sis, maybe there's something God is nudging you to do — or stop doing. Maybe it's your words, your tone, your attitude, your willingness to forgive, or even how you pray for your husband. We can't complain and disobey and still expect victory. Obedience opens the door for God to move. Follow what He's asking. Trust His way — it's always better. He wants to be in the midst of your marriage, but He won't bless what you're unwilling to surrender.

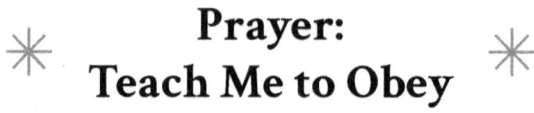

Prayer:
Teach Me to Obey

Father, in Jesus' name, I ask that You lovingly lead my sister to repentance so she can have a mind and a heart to obey Your instructions. Show her that her way will not work — but *Your* way will lead her to victory in her marriage. Reveal anything that's blocking her from hearing You and obeying You fully. Remind her that her marriage is holy ground and You want to dwell in the midst of it. Bind anything that tries to hinder her from walking in Your truth. In Jesus' name, Amen.

Reflect and Worship

♫ Song Suggestion:
"Yes"
— Shekinah Glory Ministry

Sis, as you listen, let this time of worship encourage you to lay down every excuse and hesitation. Open your heart wide and embrace what God is calling you to do. *Look it up on your favorite music platform and let it inspire your spirit today.*

Reflection Prompt:

Are there areas where you've been complaining but still expecting victory? Has the Father given you instructions you haven't yet obeyed? What's holding you back — and what step can you take today to fully say *yes?*

Day 12:   Did You Ask God?

Scripture:
"But when the people of Gibeon heard what Joshua had done to Jericho and Ai, they resorted to deception to save themselves... So the Israelites examined their food, but they did not consult the Lord."
— *Joshua 9:3–4, 14 (NLT)*

Dear Sis,

Sis, when you can, go back and read the entire chapter of Joshua 9 — it's a story we can all relate to. It's almost funny how we still do the same thing today: we come up with our own plans without asking God first.

How many times have I done this? *Plenty.* Why do we do it? For me, it was usually because I lacked trust in God in certain areas of my marriage or life. Maybe I didn't think He'd move fast enough, or maybe I thought I had a better idea — but Sis, the truth is, we never do.

We must include God in *everything* — especially in our marriages. We don't know what's ahead. We don't know the motives of every person who tries to speak into our marriages. We don't know how the enemy might try to slip in through small decisions or connections. But God sees it all.

Including Him will save your marriage unnecessary heartache. It'll keep you from making agreements you shouldn't make — whether with people, business deals, or even words spoken over your husband. It'll help you guard your heart and your home.

Sis, we can do better. We *must* do better. Make it your daily habit to stop and ask God, *"What do You think? Should I say yes to this? Should I move forward? Should I wait?"* And then — here's the part we forget — *wait for His answer.*

When we include Him, we're covered. And our marriages will be stronger for it.

Prayer:
Speak, Lord!

Father, as my sister goes back and reads this whole chapter, give her fresh insight for her own life and her marriage. Open her eyes to see any hidden plots, plans, or deceptions that could affect her home. Teach her to pause and consult You about everything — big or small. Give her ears to hear Your voice and a heart to wait for Your answer. May her obedience keep her home covered and strong. In Jesus' name, Amen.

Reflect and Worship

♬ Song Suggestion:
"I Need Thee"
— Bishop Paul S. Morton

Sis, let this worship time remind you just how much you need Him—for every decision and every moment of your day. *Find it on your favorite music platform and let it deepen your connection with God today.*

Reflection Prompt:

What areas of your marriage have you been managing on your own? Where do you need to pause, invite God in, and wait for His direction?

_____

_____

_____

_____

_____

_____

_____

_____

_____

_____

_____

_____

_____

_____

_____

_____

_____

_____

_____

_____

_____

_____

_____

Day 13: Wait on It — It's Coming

Scripture:
"Not one of the good promises which the Lord had spoken to the house of Israel failed; all had come to pass."
— Joshua 21:45 (AMP)

Dear Sis,

You can count on it — if God spoke it, He will do it. *Wait on it. Wait on Him. It's coming.*

Sis, I know God has spoken promises to you about your marriage — things He whispered to you in prayer, maybe even things you haven't told anyone else because they feel too big or too impossible. I want to encourage you today: hold on. If He said it, He *will* do it.

God will not fail you. *He hasn't failed you.* Every promise He made to Israel came to pass — and every promise He's made to you will too. He's the same faithful God.

I know waiting can feel long. I know you may be asking, *When, Lord?* — but the truth is, only He knows the right time. And Sis, His timing is *perfect.* While you wait, keep your heart soft and your faith strong. Keep believing Him about your marriage, even when it looks like nothing is changing. Keep speaking life over your husband, even when it's hard.

If you can, share what God has promised with your husband — invite him to stand in agreement with you in prayer. There is power in unity. When a husband and wife stand together on God's Word, mountains move.

Don't take matters into your own hands trying to "make it happen." That never ends well — trust me, I've tried. Stay in position. Keep praying. Keep praising. Keep expecting. You will see it come to pass, and when you do, you'll look back and thank God you didn't give up while you waited.

Prayer:
Strength to Wait

Father, thank You for every promise You have spoken over my sister's life and marriage. Give her strength to hold on while she waits for You to do what only You can do. Cover her, her husband, and their marriage in this season of waiting. Speak fresh revelation to her heart and remind her that Your timing is perfect. Let her look back at this season one day and see that every moment of waiting was worth it. Keep her faith strong and her hope alive. In Jesus' name, Amen.

Reflect and Worship

♫ Song Suggestion:
"Promises"
— Maverick City Music (feat. Joe L. Barnes & Naomi Raine)

Sis, let this worship moment encourage your heart and remind you that God's promises are sure and steadfast — just like His love for you. *Look it up on your favorite music platform and let it uplift your spirit today.*

Reflection Prompt:

What are some of the promises God has spoken to you about your marriage? Write them down and pray over them today, trusting Him to bring them to pass in His perfect time.

Day 14: Do Your Part — Take Control of Your Mind

Scripture:
"Finally, believers, whatever is true, whatever is honorable and worthy of respect, whatever is right and confirmed by God's word, whatever is pure and wholesome, whatever is lovely and brings peace, whatever is admirable and of good repute; if there is any excellence, if there is anything worthy of praise, think continually on these things [center your mind on them, and implant them in your heart]."
— Philippians 4:8 (AMP)

Dear Sis,

Sis, I treat Scripture like medicine — and this scripture right here is a powerful prescription for your mind. Take it daily.

There will be moments when your mind wants to run wild with worry, fear, or negative thoughts about your marriage. Maybe you're replaying an argument. Maybe you're stressed about what hasn't changed yet. Maybe you're wondering if it's ever going to get better. Sis, at that moment — *take your medicine.*

God's Word says you can choose what you think about. Worrying won't fix it — but worship will. Stressing won't heal it — but meditating on what is true, lovely, and praiseworthy *will* strengthen you to stand.

When your thoughts want to spiral, pause and ask the Holy Spirit to help you focus on what is good. Think about the things you love about your husband. Think about the ways God has been faithful in your marriage before. Think about the blessings that sometimes get buried under frustration.

Marriage is beautiful — but like any living thing, it has its seasons. Some seasons feel easy and light; others stretch you and grow you. In those harder seasons, you have to discipline your mind to stay focused on what is good.

Do your part: guard your thoughts. Choose what you dwell on. The enemy would love to plant seeds of doubt, fear, and resentment in your mind — but you have the authority to reject them. Take your thoughts captive, Sis, and speak life instead.

Prayer: Guard My Mind

Father, I pray that You cover my sister's mind today. When her thoughts are tempted to dwell on the negative things in her marriage, remind her to take her spiritual medicine — Your Word. Teach her to center her mind on what is true, lovely, and worthy of praise. Help her to see the good in her husband and in her home, and to trust that You are working, even when she can't see it. Keep her thoughts in perfect peace. In Jesus' name, Amen.

Reflect and Worship

♫ Song Suggestion:
"Holy Spirit"
— Eddie James

Sis, let this worship inspire you to invite the Holy Spirit's presence to guard your thoughts and fill your mind with peace. *Look it up on your favorite music platform and let it soothe your heart today.*

Reflection Prompt:

What are three things you deeply love about your husband and your marriage? Write them down and thank God for them today.

Day 15: Speak His Word

Scripture:
"God is not a man, that He should lie,
Nor a son of man, that He should repent.
Has He said, and will He not do it?
Or has He spoken and will He not make it good and fulfill it?"
— Numbers 23:19 (AMP)

Dear Sis,

Sis, God's Word is not just ink on paper — it's living, powerful, and true. He is not like people. He doesn't change His mind, He doesn't lie, and He doesn't make empty promises. If He said it — He *will* do it.

This is why it's so important for you to *speak His Word* over your marriage. When things look the opposite of what God promised, open your mouth and declare what *He* says, not what your situation says.

Maybe you're believing for restoration, deeper intimacy, healing of old wounds, or for your husband to grow spiritually — whatever it is, find a promise in His Word and speak it.

When doubt tries to creep in, open your mouth. When fear whispers, *It'll never change,* answer it back with His Word: *"God is not a man that He should lie. If He said it, He will do it."*

Sis, your words have power. Life and death are in the power of your tongue. What you speak over your husband, your home, and your marriage matters. Even when it feels like nothing is shifting, keep planting those seeds of truth.

Speak blessings when you want to complain. Speak peace when there's tension. Speak hope when you feel discouraged. God honors His Word — and He will watch over it to perform it.

Prayer:

Help Me Declare Your Truth

Father, thank You that every word You speak is true and will not return empty. Remind my sister to open her mouth and declare Your promises over her marriage daily. Give her faith to believe that what You said, You will do — in Your time and Your way. Help her reject fear and doubt, and to stand firm on what You've spoken. Let her words line up with Your Word so her marriage can flourish and bring You glory. In Jesus' name, Amen.

Reflect and Worship

♫ Song Suggestion:
"Atmosphere Shift"
— Phil Thompson

Sis, as you worship, let this moment stir your faith and shift the atmosphere in your mind, your heart, and your home. Open your mouth and boldly speak God's Word over your marriage — and trust that as you do, things are changing even now. *Find it on your favorite music platform and let it strengthen your faith today.*

Reflection Prompt:

What promise from God's Word do you need to declare over your marriage today? Write it down, speak it out loud, and stand on it until you see it fulfilled.

Day 16:   Equipped by God

Scripture:
"So I am well pleased with weaknesses, with insults, with distresses, with persecutions, and with difficulties, for the sake of Christ; for when I am weak [in human strength], then I am strong [truly able, truly powerful, truly drawing from God's strength]."
— 2 Corinthians 12:10 (AMP)

Dear Sis,

Sis, there are times I look back at some of the things I've accomplished and I *know* it was God equipping me with what I needed. When I need to draw strength from Him, I remind myself of all the times He has carried me through.

We all have our moments. Sometimes you just want to give up. Sometimes you want to quit. But those are exactly the times when you need to draw from God's strength. He promises He will never leave you nor forsake you. He will be right there when you need Him most.

Sis, I want to encourage you to draw on His strength to love your husband when it feels hard. And when it feels easy — rest. Draw on His strength to be patient while He does a good work in you *and* in your husband.

After every success, rest. Give yourself and your husband the grace to grow as God nudges, shapes, and loves you both. You and your husband deserve His grace.

So when something feels hard or challenging, go back and read this scripture to remind yourself that God will strengthen you — for your husband, for your family, and for His glory. I know you can do it, Sis — and it *will be* worth it. Stick with it!

Prayer:
Strengthen Me, Lord

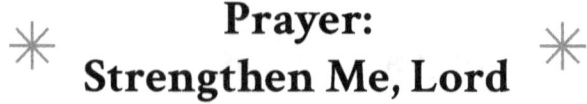

Father, in Jesus' name, I pray for my sister — strengthen her for every task You've placed before her. When she feels weak or wants to give up, remind her that You are right there with her. When challenges come, help her run to You in prayer and draw strength for whatever she's facing. Father, give her strategy, give her a plan, and anoint her steps. In Jesus' name, Amen.

Reflect and Worship

🎵 **Song Suggestion:**
"Great Are You Lord"
— Casting Crowns

Sis, as you worship today, remember that even in your weakness, God is strong. Let this song remind you that He is the source of your strength and the One who equips you daily. *Find it on your favorite music platform and let it refresh your spirit today.*

Reflection Prompt:

Take a moment to write a prayer for your husband — and come back to it whenever you need a reminder that God is equipping you both, every step of the way.

Day 17:   Don't Give Up

Scripture:
"Let us not grow weary or become discouraged in doing good, for at the proper time we will reap, if we do not give in."
— *Galatians 6:9 (AMP)*

Dear Sis,

Sis, now is not the time to throw in the towel. Now is not the time to give up. Now is not the time to listen to the enemy's lies. Now is not the time to stop going to church. Now is not the time to stop believing for a miracle in your marriage. Now is not the time to stop praying for your husband. Now is not the time. Not now.

Keep going. Keep pushing. I'm proud of you. God is smiling on you. God loves you.

I understand that marriage has its ups and downs. Trust me, I know. There were moments when I wanted to give up and walk away — but Sis, I am so glad I didn't. I'm so thankful God gave me the strength to hold on and keep pressing forward.

The enemy would love nothing more than for you to give up on your husband and abandon your marriage emotionally or even physically. But God's Word encourages us to keep doing good, because in due season, we *will* reap if we do not give up. One day, you'll look back and thank God you didn't quit.

Whatever season you're in right now, go to God in prayer and lay it all at His feet. He already knows, but He still wants to hear from you. He wants to guide you. He wants to anoint you. It all starts when you commit to going to Him and giving Him your heart and your marriage. Let Him fill you with what you need for this season.

I believe it will get better. I am praying for you, Sis. Don't give up. Your marriage is worth it. Your husband is worth it. Fight in the Spirit and watch God bring forth what is needed in your marriage, in your husband, and in you.

Prayer:
Strength to Keep Going

Father, in Jesus' name, I pray for my sister. Give her strength, peace, love, patience, and anointing to love her husband even in difficult seasons. Thank You for equipping her with the tools and strategies to cover herself and her marriage. Thank You for reminding her that this is just a season — and this too shall pass. I decree and declare breakthrough in her marriage in Jesus' name. Cover her emotions, and by the authority given to me through Jesus Christ, I come against every spirit that comes to weary her. In Jesus' name, Amen.

Reflect and Worship

🎵 **Song Suggestion:**
"Rest on Us" (feat. Brandon Lake & Eniola Abioye)
— Maverick City Music & UPPERROOM

Sis, as you worship, invite the Holy Spirit to come into your home and your marriage. Let this song remind you that He is with you, strengthening you for this journey and surrounding your marriage with His presence. *Find it on your favorite music platform and let it speak to your heart today.*

Reflection Prompt:

What season are you in right now? What are you believing God for in this season? Write it out and give it back to Him today.

Day 18: Get Up, Now It Is Not the Time to Lay Down!

Scripture:
"And He got up and [sternly] rebuked the wind and said to the sea, 'Hush, be still (muzzled)!' And the wind died down [as if it had grown weary] and there was [at once] a great calm [a perfect peacefulness]."
— Mark 4:39 (AMP)

Dear Sis,

Sis, as we go through challenges and face tough circumstances, we're often tempted to sit down — or even lay down — in defeat. Trust me, I understand! There have been so many times I wanted to crawl into bed, pull the covers over my head, cry, and close the curtains until everything somehow fixed itself.

We feel like giving up for so many reasons. Maybe you're tired of the warfare — fighting in the Spirit for your marriage and feeling worn out. I understand, Sis. Maybe you're weary from believing for a miracle and a breakthrough while watching everyone else get theirs. And you sit there wondering, *When is it my time?* Sis, I understand.

When the enemy starts speaking to you — lying to you — whispering that your circumstances may never change, that is the moment you need to get up. That's right. Get up, Sis. Get up and rebuke the enemy. Tell him to hush. Speak victory into your life, your marriage, your husband, and your family. Choose to fight. Choose not to give up. Do not let the enemy win in your life.

God has given you — His daughter — power and authority. Walk in your authority, Sis. Use it. This is not the time to lay down in defeat. Get up. I know you're tired. I know you've been believing. But keep praying. Keep believing. Keep declaring victory over your marriage. Don't choose defeat — choose victory!

I'm standing with you in faith. I believe you will see breakthrough. I believe your marriage will be stronger than ever. Get up, Sis — and speak peace to every storm.

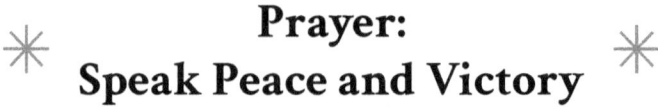

Prayer: Speak Peace and Victory

Father, in Jesus' name, I declare and decree that my sister will live and not die and declare the works of the Lord. Father, I speak life into her and her circumstances. Give her strength for her marriage. Give her the words to speak to her husband to build him up. Give her peace when stress tries to bombard her mind. I thank You for my sister choosing not to give up but to keep going. In Jesus' name, Amen.

Reflect and Worship

♫ Song Suggestion:
"Raise a Hallelujah"
— Yolanda Stith & Strong City

Sis, as you worship, boldly speak victory over your situation. Declare victory over every storm in your life and remind yourself that you carry His authority. Get up, stand firm, and speak breakthrough and miracles until peace fills your heart. *Find this song on your favorite music platform and let it wash over you today.*

Reflection Prompt:

Sis, take a deep breath. Write a letter to yourself today. Encourage yourself with words you need to hear and remind yourself that you have the strength to get up and keep going.

Day 19:   Forgiveness

Scripture:

"Whenever you stand praying, if you have anything against anyone, forgive him [drop the issue, let it go], so that your Father who is in heaven will also forgive you your transgressions and wrongdoings [against Him and others]. But if you do not forgive, neither will your Father in heaven forgive your transgressions."
— *Mark 11:25–26 (AMP)*

Dear Sis,

Sis, I love reading this verse from the Amplified Bible. It defines forgiveness so clearly: *drop the issue and let it go.* Whew. That's a lot, right? Let's be real — sometimes, you don't want to let it go. Sometimes, you want to hold on to what was said, what was done, and how it made you feel. And sometimes... we do. But the Word of God makes it plain: *Drop the issue. Let it go.*

Now Sis, while you're walking through the emotions of forgiveness, remember to give yourself grace. It's okay to feel what you feel — but don't stay there. Don't unpack and build a home in hurt or offense. Invite God into those hard places. He will walk with you through it if you'll let Him. Sometimes we just don't understand why people do what they do or say what they say. And we want to understand. Trust me, I've tried. But trying to understand the issues in someone else's heart can sometimes lead us into a deeper pit — one that's filled with resentment and unforgiveness.

Sis, in marriage, you will go through some things. Remember those vows you spoke in that beautiful dress — *for better or for worse, in sickness and in health?* Marriage brings many opportunities for grace, and forgiveness is one we're called to choose again and again. Now hear me clearly — I'm not saying you should allow mistreatment or abuse. What I am saying is this: forgive, heal, and let our Heavenly Father handle it all. Forgiveness doesn't mean approval — it means freedom. Your freedom. Your healing. Your peace.

God doesn't want you walking around carrying the weight of past wounds. He wants you free to love your husband and your family the way He loves you — unhindered, whole, and full of grace. Sis, drop the issue... and let it go.

✳ Prayer: ✳
Healing Through Forgiveness

Father, in Jesus' name, I pray that You will heal my sister's heart and give her the strength to forgive so she can be who You've called her to be. Heal her so she can love again. Heal her so she has the strength to get up and walk in newness. Let her feel Your presence every step of the way. Show her how she looks when she's free, whole, and filled with Your peace — and give her the fight to get there. Lord, give her divine strategy for this season and remind her she is not alone. Strengthen her not to give up on herself, her marriage, or her family. In Jesus' name, Amen.

Reflect and Worship

♫ **Song Suggestion:**
"Nothing Else"
— Cody Carnes

Sis, let this song lead you into a place of surrender. As you listen, lay everything at the Father's feet — the hurt, the questions, the disappointment. Let Him meet you in that space and fill your heart with healing. *Find it on your favorite music platform and take time to simply be with Him today.*

Reflection Prompt:

What is on your heart right now after reading this? Write a letter to your Heavenly Father and tell Him how you feel. Be honest. Be open. Give it all to Him.

Day 20:   You Are Not Alone

Scripture:

"It is the Lord who goes before you; He will be with you. He will not fail you or abandon you. Do not fear or be dismayed."
— Deuteronomy 31:8 (AMP)

Dear Sis,

I want to encourage you today and remind you: you are not alone. God is with you, your husband, and your marriage. You are covered. You are seen. You are blessed.

There are some challenges we face as wives that make it feel like we're walking through the fire by ourselves. But Sis — that is a lie straight from the enemy. He wants you to believe you're isolated so that you'll abandon your marriage emotionally, or even physically. Don't believe the lie!

I've been there. I found myself in a season where I allowed what I saw to shake me. Instead of leaning into the promises of God, I let fear discourage me. I pulled back when God was asking me to press in. I resisted when He was calling me to love deeper. Sis, there were things in my heart that needed healing — and only God could do it.

I love my husband dearly, but he's not my healer. Only God can do the deep purging our souls sometimes need. And when we don't allow God to tend to those places, we can end up feeling broken, abandoned, and alone.

But the truth is, Sis — you are never alone. God is with you in every season. He's present in every tear, every prayer, every silent hope. Invite Him in. Don't leave God out of your challenges, your marriage, or your family. He wants to walk with you, hold you, and fill you with peace — every step of the way.

Prayer:
God, Reassure Her Heart

Father, in Jesus' name, strengthen my sister and heal her in every area that needs Your touch. Reassure her that she is never alone — that You are walking with her, covering her, and fighting for her marriage. Lord, I speak Jesus over her heart, her thoughts, and her home. I bind the spirit of fear, and I loose Your peace over her mind and spirit. She will not be bound. I declare and decree that she is free. In Jesus' name, Amen.

Reflect and Worship

♬ Song Suggestion:
"Gratitude"
— Brandon Lake

Sis, let this song be your worship cry today. Sometimes all we have to offer is a hallelujah — and that's more than enough. As you listen, thank God for being with you through every high and low. Let the spirit of gratefulness rise in your heart and chase away every lie of loneliness. *Find it on your favorite music platform and let it wash over you.*

Reflection Prompt:

What are some scriptures you can write down and reflect on to remind you that you are never alone? Let them become your strength when your heart feels weary.

Day 21:   Faith—Your Title Deed

Scripture:

Now faith is the assurance (title deed, confirmation) of things hoped for (divinely guaranteed), and the evidence of things not seen [the conviction of their reality—faith comprehends as fact what cannot be experienced by the physical senses].
— Hebrews 11:1 (AMP)

Dear Sis,

Do you realize that your faith is the assurance of everything God has spoken to you and all that you are believing Him for? Sis, did you catch that? This verse says that *faith is your title deed and confirmation.* Hallelujah! That gives me so much joy.

Think about this—if you had the title deed to your vehicle in your hand, you wouldn't question whether or not it's yours. You'd know it *belongs* to you. That's how it works with faith! Your *faith-title deed* is your evidence that it's already done. It's already yours. It's tangible in the spirit. Glory to God!

Grab hold of that truth, sis—and don't let go. By faith, every promise of God is yours. Walk through His Word and highlight His promises concerning your marriage. Then declare and decree them over your life and home.

This scripture makes me leap for joy because I think about the things the Lord has shown me—through dreams, visions, and whispered words—and I hold them in my heart like they're already in my hands. That's faith. I believe and receive before I ever see it with my natural eyes.

One more thing, sis—keep your *hope* alive. The enemy would love for your hope to die so you'll give up and stop believing. But the devil is a liar! Believe God. Hold on to your faith and keep your hope burning. Everything He has shown you will come to pass.

Prayer:
Faith Revival

Father, in Jesus' name, I declare and decree a revival in my sister's spirit. Revive her mind, her heart, and her walk with You. I thank You that her hope will never die and that joy will be her portion. Thank You for doing a new thing in her heart, in her husband's heart, and in their marriage. Every promise You've shown her will come to pass. In Jesus' name, amen.

Reflect and Worship

♫ Song Suggestion:
"Been So Good"
— Tiffany Hudson

Sis, let this worship song remind you of how faithful God has already been—and stir your faith for what's still coming. He's not done. Your title deed is in your hands!

Reflection Prompt:

Take a moment and write down a few things you are believing God for in your marriage. Then, speak over them by faith—your title deed says they are already yours.

Day 22:   An Ear to Hear

Scripture:
Anyone with ears to hear must listen to the Spirit and understand what he is saying to the churches. To everyone who is victorious I will give fruit from the tree of life in the paradise of God.
— *Revelation 2:7 NLT*

Dear Sis,

Let me share something personal with you—I often pray this verse over my family. It's one I cling to because I deeply desire that we all keep an ear tuned to the Lord. I don't want us swayed by our flesh or the enemy's lies, but instead to hear clearly what the Spirit is saying.

This is especially important to me for my husband—as the priest of our home, I pray that he not only listens to the Spirit but truly hears, reflects, and obeys. Sis, I don't want him to just hear and move on—I want him to marinate in God's Word and follow the Spirit's leading with confidence and humility.

We're living in critical times, and having spiritual ears to hear is not optional—it's essential. I encourage you today: pray this verse over yourself, your husband, your marriage, and your family. Be the kind of wife who leans into the voice of the Holy Spirit and moves when He speaks.

Sis, spend intentional time with the Holy Spirit. He longs to whisper divine insight concerning your heart, your home, and your marriage. Remember—marriage is ministry. And the Spirit of God wants to walk with both you and your husband every step of the way.

Prayer:
Give Me Ears to Hear

Father, in Jesus' name, I pray that my sister will make space to know the Holy Spirit in a new and personal way. Let her ears be sensitive to Your voice and her heart ready to obey. I pray she'll be led by You as she intercedes for herself and her marriage. May her union bear much fruit for Your glory. Lord, I also ask that You guard her ear gates—let nothing contaminate how she hears and moves with the Spirit. In Jesus' name, amen.

Reflect and Worship

♫ Song Suggestion:
"Mighty Name of Jesus"
— The Belonging Co & Hope Darst

Sis, let this powerful worship song stir your spirit. As you listen, ask the Holy Spirit to fine-tune your ears to hear His truth louder than any distraction. Let every word sung be a declaration over your life and your marriage.

Reflection Prompt:

In this season, what has the Holy Spirit spoken to you? How are you intentionally praying over yourself, your husband, and your marriage?

Day 23: Ask God First

Scripture:

If any of you lacks wisdom [to guide him through a decision or circumstance] he is to ask of [our benevolent] God, who gives to everyone generously and without rebuke or blame, and it will be given to him.
— — James 1:5 AMP

Dear Sis,

In life and marriage, we will face many moments that require a decision. Sometimes, it will be something you and your husband decide together; other times, it may be a choice you must make on your own. Either way, decisions will come—and the beautiful truth is, we don't have to figure them out alone. God is ready to assist, support, and guide us... all we have to do is ask.

Our Father is full of wisdom, so why try to navigate things in our own strength? There's such peace in knowing that He's always ready to listen and lead us through any circumstance. I remember a time in my marriage that was emotionally difficult for me. It was a decision I couldn't make with my husband, but I knew I needed God's wisdom more than anything. I fasted, prayed, and sought His direction—not wanting to act from my flesh but to be led by the Holy Spirit. And sis, God showed up. He gave me the answer I *needed*, not the one I *wanted*. I thank Him for that. Hallelujah!

This verse reminds us that when we ask, He gives generously—without shame or blame. Let's make it our habit to go to God first, letting Him guide every decision and circumstance. No need to walk through it alone, sis. We've got help.

Prayer:
Father, Give Us Wisdom

Father, in Jesus' name, I thank You for Your Word and Your wisdom. Guide my sister in whatever she's facing today and give her the wisdom she needs. Lord, we can't do life or marriage without You—and we know that. As she runs to You, fill her with Your love, power, strength, and grace so she can stay committed to the assignments You have placed in her hands. In Jesus' name, Amen.

Reflect and Worship

♫ Song Suggestion:
"I Give Myself Away"
— William McDowell

Sis, this song is a beautiful reminder that when we surrender ourselves fully to God, He can lead us into the very best path. Take a quiet moment, listen, and let the lyrics be your prayer today. *Look it up on your favorite music platform.*

Reflection Prompt:

What are the areas in your life and marriage right now where you need God's wisdom and guidance? Write them down and pray over each one, asking Him to lead you.

Day 24: There Is a Way

Scripture:

Understand this, my beloved brothers and sisters. Let everyone be quick to hear [be a careful, thoughtful listener], slow to speak [a speaker of carefully chosen words], slow to anger [patient, reflective, forgiving]; for the [resentful, deep-seated] anger of man does not produce the righteousness of God [that standard of behavior which He requires from us].
— James 1:19–20 AMP

Dear Sis,

There were times I allowed my emotions to get in the way of how I listened and spoke to my husband. God dealt with me about it, and my husband communicated to me that he didn't like it. I had to really do better—and guess what? I really wanted to. Just as much as I want to be heard, I wanted my husband to feel heard as well.

Honestly, as I began to seek God for His help and His way, He showed me where I picked it up from and how I carried it into my marriage. In marriage, husbands and wives should invite this way of communicating so we can create a safe place to land. We all deserve to be heard, and we also deserve to have the opportunity to speak knowing our spouses are listening.

Thank God the Bible describes a way of doing it right—quick to listen and slow to speak! This strategy is for everyone to follow, and it truly helps create, grow, and mature all relationships, especially in marriage. Sis, I encourage you to go back and read the scriptures again. Let God speak to you and show you how you can improve. Don't be afraid to invite God in so He can show you yourself. We all have to walk out our own soul salvation, so let's choose to do it right.

Prayer:
Quick to Listen, Slow to Speak

Father, in Jesus' name, I cover my sister in prayer as she comes to You seeking Your help to have a mindset to be quick to listen and slow to speak. Father, let this flow through her and allow her husband and family to reap the benefits. I pray that her husband will be willing to be quick to listen and slow to speak as well. Through both of them having this mindset, may they heal together, break generational curses, and kick the enemy out of their marriage in every way. In Jesus' name, amen.

Reflect and Worship

🎵 Song Suggestion:
"Open the Eyes of My Heart"
— Jordan G. Welch

Sis, this worship song is such a heartfelt prayer. As you listen, ask God to help you love and respond in His way within your marriage. *Look it up on your favorite music platform and let it minister to you.*

Reflection Prompt:

Do you see areas where you or your husband need to be quicker to listen and slower to speak? If so, lay it down right here in prayer to your Heavenly Father, and leave it with Him, knowing He will help both of you communicate more effectively.

Day 25:   Surrender

Scripture:
O Lord, I give my life to you.
— Psalm 25:1 NLT

Dear Sis,

In marriage, there will be moments when your spouse may hurt you—intentionally or unintentionally. There will be challenges of all kinds. Let me be real with you: during a season of blending family challenges, I had to completely surrender both the situation and my emotions to the Lord.

I remember growing frustrated because things weren't coming together at the pace I wanted. One moment I'd be okay, and the next, frustration would creep back in. Eventually, I realized I was exhausting myself, trying to manage it all in my own strength. The best decision I made in that moment was to give it all to Jesus—my anger, my frustration, my timeline...everything.

Are you facing a challenge like that right now? Sis, the more I walk with the Lord, the more I recognize there are areas I must surrender to Him. These are often the very areas that tempt me to react as if I don't have a Savior. When I catch myself overthinking, doubting, worrying, or feeling stressed, this scripture reminds me: *Surrender* it.

Sis, whatever is weighing on your heart or mind—give it to Jesus. He can handle it far better than you can. Holding on to it will only drain you, especially knowing we serve a God who has promised to take care of us. So, let it go. Surrender it all.

Prayer:
Help Me Surrender, Lord

Father God, in the name of Jesus, I ask that You cover my sister in Your love and remind her that she doesn't have to carry it alone. When she chooses to surrender her life, challenges, and situations to You, fill her with Your peace and wisdom. Father, we can do nothing apart from You—and we don't want to. Lead and guide my sister on her journey with You. In Jesus' name, Amen.

Reflect and Worship

🎵 Song Suggestion:
"Tired"
—Todd Galberth

Sis, if you're feeling worn out from carrying things that were never yours to bear, this song will minister to your spirit. Let it remind you that it's okay to lay it all at His feet. *Find it on your favorite music platform.*

Reflection Prompt:

What are some things you need to surrender to your Father right now? Write them down, pray over them, and release them into His hands today.

Day 26:   Take It to God

Scripture:
Give all your worries and cares to God, for he cares about you.
— 1 Peter 5:7 NLT

Dear Sis,

In the last entry, we talked about surrendering every challenge and situation. That's vital! But today, I want to take it a step further and encourage you to live with a mindset that says: *Take it to Jesus.*

In your marriage—and in every area of life—whatever has you overthinking, worrying, or feeling stressed, take it straight to God.

He already has the answers. He holds the solutions. He knows the beginning and the end. There's no need to waste precious time trying to figure it all out when your Heavenly Father already knows.

Sis, the key is to trust God. Relax—He's got you. I've had to trust Him with my marriage, and I still do. I've had to trust Him with my children, and I still do. When I catch myself overthinking a situation in my marriage, I take it to my Father in prayer. Each time I do, I feel lighter. It frees my mind and hands to focus on the things He *does* want me to work on in that moment.

The moment trials or challenges come your way, take them to God—and leave them there. Don't pick them back up. Hallelujah!

Prayer:
I'm Bringing It All to You, Lord

Father, in Jesus' name, I lift up my sister, her marriage, and her family. Whatever she is facing, whatever she is going through—work it out for her good. Help her bring *everything* to You, knowing that only You have the final say. I speak peace over every situation in her life and marriage. In Jesus' name, Amen.

Reflect and Worship

♫ Song Suggestion:
"My Life Is in Your Hands"
—Kirk Franklin & God's Property

Sis, let this song remind you that you don't have to figure it all out or carry it all on your own. Your life is safe in His hands. Find it on your favorite music platform.

Reflection Prompt:

What are some things you are taking to God right now so that He can have the final say? Write them down and release them into His care.

Day 27: Don't Give Up on Your Dreams and God's Promises

Scripture:

So let's not get tired of doing what is good. At just the right time we will reap a harvest of blessing if we don't give up.
— Galatians 6:9 NLT

Dear Sis,

Think about the dreams in your heart and the promises God has spoken over your life. Don't wait until everything "lines up" to start moving forward—go with God's leading and His grace. Giving up is not an option.

As wives, we often put ourselves last for so many reasons. I know I did for years. One of my lifelong dreams was to become an author, but I kept putting it off. Then one day, I decided to finally do what I had always envisioned myself doing. It wasn't easy—it took planning, late nights, and persistence—but by God's grace, I did it!

Sis, I want to encourage you to pray about your next steps and follow God's direction. And when it comes to your marriage, don't give up on what God has promised you there, either. His Word is full of promises, and you can claim them for your relationship. There may also be personal promises God has spoken directly to you—hold on to those.

No matter what it looks like, keep being your husband's wife. Keep going. Keep praying. Keep believing. It will get better.

Prayer:
Strength to Keep Going

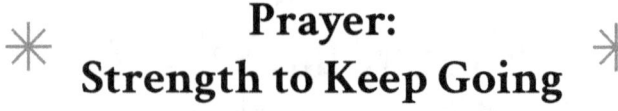

Father God, in the name of Jesus, give my sister strength to keep moving forward no matter what she sees. Remind her of Your many promises and that You are a promise-keeping God. Show her how to walk out the dreams You've placed in her heart, and give her the grace and anointing to do all You've called her to do. In Jesus' name, Amen.

Reflect and Worship

♫ Song Suggestion:
"For My Good"
— Maverick City Music & Chandler Moore feat. Todd Galberth

Sis, this song will remind you that God always has a plan even when you can't see it yet. *Find it on your favorite music platform.*

Reflection Prompt:

Write down your dreams and the promises of God you're holding on to. Keep them in a place where you can revisit them, so when they come to pass, you'll see the track record of His faithfulness.

Day 28:   Keep Your Eyes Open

Scripture:
Stay alert. Watch out for your great enemy, the devil. He prowls around like a roaring lion, looking for someone to devour.
— 1 Peter 5:8 NLT

Dear Sis,

Don't think the enemy doesn't notice your desire to live right. He sees that you want to be the wife God has called you to be. He sees you and your husband growing closer to God and to each other. He sees your prayers, your faith, and your focus. And because of that, he will try everything he can to distract you.

But sis, hear me—you are doing a good job. You're staying focused, you're pressing forward, you're growing closer to God, and you're praying more than ever before. That's exactly why the enemy wants to stop you. He does not want you and your husband communicating effectively. He does not want to see your love grow stronger. He wants to bring division. He wants to bring fear. And he will try to use anyone or anything around you to steal your focus.

Stay alert. Keep pushing. If you need help, don't be afraid to reach out. Find someone you can trust who is for your marriage—someone who wants to see you and your husband win. Get a prayer partner. Be determined to pray down strongholds and break generational curses in Jesus' name.

The enemy will not destroy your marriage or your family. Why? Because God always wins. Stay connected to Him, keep your eyes open, and let His wisdom, knowledge, and understanding guide you. Don't give in to fear—lean into God.

Prayer:
Eyes Open, Heart Anchored

Father, in Jesus' name, I come against every demonic attack against my sister's marriage and family. Open her eyes to recognize the enemy's tactics, and open her ears so she may clearly hear Your voice. Cover her mind and heart so she does not give in to fear but walks in Your wisdom and strength. I declare that her marriage and her family are covered by the blood of Jesus, and I speak victory over her household. In Jesus' name, Amen.

Reflect and Worship

♫ Song Suggestion:
"Firm Foundation"
—Cody Carnes

Sis, let this song remind you that no matter what the enemy throws your way, your marriage and your life are built on Christ, the solid rock. Find it on your favorite music platform.

Reflection Prompt:

Has the Lord revealed to you areas where you need to remain diligent in prayer concerning your marriage and family? Write them down and create a prayer plan to stay consistent in covering those areas.

Day 29: Just Keep Living!

Scripture:

It is God's will that your honorable lives should silence those ignorant people who make foolish accusations against you.

— — 1 Peter 2:15 NLT

Dear Sis,

That's right—just keep living! People are going to be people, whether they are saved or not. Some will talk about you, your husband, and your marriage whether things are going well or not. But here's the truth: your life and your marriage, when surrendered to God, will speak louder than any words others may say.

Sis, don't let the enemy pull you into distraction through gossip, criticism, or opinions that don't matter. It's all noise. And noise is meant to break your focus. But you don't have to answer to anyone but Jesus. Keep living with integrity. Keep loving your husband. Keep covering your family in prayer. Over time, your consistency, your faith, and your obedience to God will silence the voices of opposition.

Sometimes the best response is not a response at all—it's your life. Keep living with joy. Keep living with honor. Keep living in a way that glorifies God. Your walk will testify louder than your words ever could. And remember, when you feel weighed down by distractions, go back to the One who gives you strength. He'll give you peace and remind you that His opinion is the only one that matters.

Prayer:
Focused on You, Lord

Father, in the name of Jesus, I ask that You help my sister keep living for You and stay focused on pleasing You above all else. When distractions, gossip, or criticism come her way, remind her that her worth and her marriage are in Your hands. Give her strength, wisdom, and strategies to rise above the noise and live in a way that glorifies You. In Jesus' name, Amen.

Reflect and Worship

♫ Song Suggestion:
"My Life Is in Your Hands"
—God's Property

Sis, let this song remind you that no matter what others say or think, your life and marriage are safe in God's hands. His opinion is the one that counts. Find it on your favorite music platform.

Reflection Prompt:

What are some areas where you find yourself getting distracted concerning your marriage and family? Write them down, and then ask God to help you release those distractions and focus on Him.

Day 30: Rest in God

Scripture:

Be still in the presence of the Lord, and wait patiently for him to act. Don't worry about evil people who prosper or fret about their wicked schemes. Stop being angry! Turn from your rage! Do not lose your temper— it only leads to harm. For the wicked will be destroyed, but those who trust in the Lord will possess the land.
— Psalm 37:7–9 NLT

Dear Sis,

Challenges in marriage will come, and they can frustrate you or stir up anger if you're not careful. But these are the very moments when God calls us to *be still in His presence.* Instead of reacting quickly out of emotion, bring the situation to Him and let Him guide you in how to respond.

Anger can make us say things we don't mean or do things that damage what God is working to heal. That's why this scripture encourages us to turn from rage and choose trust instead. Sis, God doesn't want you burdened by frustration. He wants you resting in His peace, knowing that He is fighting for you, your marriage, and your family.

Resting in God doesn't mean ignoring your challenges—it means handing them over to the One who already has the solution. It means trusting that His timing is perfect, even when it feels delayed. It means reminding yourself that your battle is not against flesh and blood, but against the enemy who wants to destroy unity.

Sis, choose peace over anger. Choose prayer over reaction. Choose to rest in God's presence and let Him give you the wisdom and patience you need. When you wait on Him, He will not only guide you—He will strengthen you.

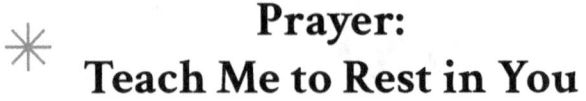

Prayer:
Teach Me to Rest in You

Father, in Jesus' name, I ask that You help my sister settle her emotions and rest in Your presence. Remind her that her anger does not produce Your righteousness, and teach her to trust You with every situation in her marriage and family. Cover her with Your peace, and give her wisdom to respond with grace, patience, and faith. In Jesus' name, Amen.

Reflect and Worship

🎵 **Song Suggestion:**
"Our God Reigns"
—Martin Smith, Kari Jobe, and Cody Carnes

Sis, let this song wash over you as a reminder that no matter what's happening around you, God reigns. He is in control, and you can rest in that truth. Find it on your favorite music platform.

Reflection Prompt:

What is heavy on your mind right now? Write it down and intentionally release it to the Lord, asking Him to give you rest and peace in exchange.

Day 31: God Is Your Strength

Scripture:

The Lord will give [unyielding and impenetrable] strength to His people;
The Lord will bless His people with peace.
— *Psalm 29:11 AMP*

Dear Sis,

When it seems like things could only get worse, when nothing feels like it's changing, or when the weight of your situation feels unbearable—pray, and then pray some more. Only God can give you the strength and peace you need to endure and make it through to the other side.

In seasons of pain, doubt, and unfair circumstances, it can feel tempting to give in to your emotions. Trust me, I know how emotions can rise up and try to take over. But in those very moments, you must choose Jesus. Let Him lead, let Him guide, and let Him carry you through.

Sis, I can't tell you how many times I've had to stop in the middle of my own frustration or weakness and make the choice to invite Jesus into that moment. Every single time, He gave me the strength I needed—not always to change the situation instantly, but to strengthen *me* while I walked through it.

Marriage is beautiful, but it requires sacrifice, submission, and yielding—not in your own strength, but in the strength of Christ. With Jesus, you can endure the hard days, celebrate the joyful ones, and grow closer to God and your spouse through it all. He will never fail you, and His strength is more than enough.

As you close this 31-day journey, remember this: you are not walking alone. God is your strength. God is your peace. And God is your guide. Keep leaning on Him, because He will always carry you through.

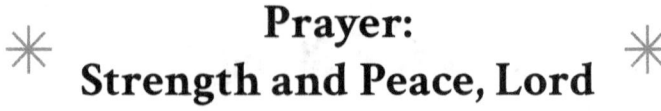

Prayer:
Strength and Peace, Lord

Father, in the name of Jesus, I thank You for being my sister's strength and her peace. When she feels weak, remind her that Your power is made perfect in weakness. When she feels overwhelmed, cover her with Your peace that passes all understanding. Strengthen her marriage, her family, and her faith. Teach her to always run to You first, knowing that with You she can endure, overcome, and thrive. In Jesus' name, Amen.

Reflect and Worship

♫ Song Suggestion:
"Same Grace"
—William Murphy

Sis, let this song remind you that the same grace God gave others to endure, overcome, and flourish is the same grace He is giving you right now. Find it on your favorite music platform.

Reflection Prompt:

Looking back over these past 31 days, what has God strengthened in you? Write down the areas where you feel stronger, and thank Him for His faithfulness. Then, write one prayer asking Him to continue carrying you forward beyond this devotional.

A Final Word — But Not Goodbye!

Scripture:
"Trust in the Lord with all your heart; do not depend on your own understanding. Seek His will in all you do, and He will show you which path to take."
—Proverbs 3:5–6 (NLT)

Dear Sis,

You made it—and I am so proud of you.

Thirty-one days ago, you chose to invest in your marriage, your heart, and your walk with God. That is no small thing. You showed up even when it was hard. You prayed even when you didn't feel like it. You pressed through even when you didn't see immediate change. Sis, that speaks volumes about your love, your faith, and the God who has been walking with you and your husband every step of the way.

This scripture has been my anchor since before I got married, and it has carried me through many seasons. Marriage will stretch you, grow you, and sometimes bring you to the end of yourself. But that's where God shows up strongest. When you don't understand—trust Him. When the path seems unclear—seek Him. He will direct your steps and guide your marriage forward.

Let this devotional be more than just a 31-day journey; let it be a foundation you can return to again and again. God isn't finished with your story, your marriage, or your growth. The same God who spoke to you on Day 1 will continue to lead you, strengthen you, and bless the covenant you and your husband share.

Sis, you are not walking this path alone. I'm praying for you, cheering for you, and believing with you that your marriage will reflect God's love, grace, and faithfulness. Keep leaning in. Keep trusting Him. Keep choosing Jesus—in every moment, in every season.

You are seen. You are loved. You are chosen.
And Sis, you've got this—because God's got both you and your marriage.

✳ **Prayer:** ✳

Father, thank You for walking with my sister on this 31-day journey. Thank You for every prayer whispered, every tear shed, every moment of hope restored. I ask that You continue to strengthen her and her marriage. Teach her to trust You fully and to seek Your will above all else. Bless her husband and cover their union with Your peace, joy, and protection. May their love grow deeper, their bond grows stronger, and their walk with You grow sweeter each day. Complete the beautiful work You've started in them, Lord, and let their marriage shine as a testimony of Your faithfulness. In Jesus' name, Amen.

www.ingramcontent.com/pod-product-compliance
Lightning Source LLC
Chambersburg PA
CBHW070357130626
46556CB00007B/3200